saigon cemetery

saigon cemetery

D. C. Berry

University of Georgia Press, Athens

811

B5342 s

To my friends with whom I lived a year,
but I will swear it was a life.

Foreword

When I read these poems I suffer from strong, mixed feelings. When I test those feelings against experience, they ring true. These poems tell truth about war. To tell the truth they naturally aim for that quality sought for and achieved by Wilfred Owen. Owen said it all for our century of wars:

> Above all, this book is not concerned with Poetry,
> The subject of it is War, and the pity of War.
> The Poetry is in the pity.

And something very much the same could preface D.C. Berry's book. He honors that intention, not flinching from hard facts, mixed feelings, not deviating from the subject and the pity of it.

Those who are looking for more settled reactions, the comfort of easy answers for the armchair, are referred elsewhere, to the pure and simple feelings, often well-expressed, of patriots and dissenters. Two sides of one common coin. The poems of these people are always easier to *appreciate*, to talk about. Since their aim is persuasion, truth is not strictly relevant. So it is that even the rage of protest against this hard strange war in Indochina is largely rhetorical. They are concerned with right and wrong, with high and mighty abstractions.

They have no inclination towards pity. Propaganda has no place for it. Pity, the outward and visible sign of charity, is neither sentimental nor rhetorical. The author of *saigon cemetery* does not deceive himself and has no wish to deceive others.

All our wars are the same. They are outwardly different in details, therefore in idiom and language. The details must be exact, the language must be accurate— as in any ritual—for the ritual to be effacious, for the single and unique experience of one time and place to become universal and timeless. There is nothing *new* to say about war. Novelty is not the point and is certainly not a virtue. What can be new, what is new here, is the poet's own voice. Berry's voice is all his own. He is traditional in his search for a form, one flexible enough to leave the language free to be itself, yet strict enough to permit the requisite self-control. Without the rigor of form no poet could speak truly of these things. It is also traditional that the point of view is that of the medic, one half step aside from the life and death of the soldier in a line outfit, the man named for generations as a *common* soldier. Since Walt Whitman tended wounded soldiers in the Civil War, most American poetry of war (in verse and in prose) has been written by those who were near and close enough to see and to suffer the worst, but never, by definition, given over wholly, body and soul, to the business of war as the combat soldier must be. John Crowe Ransom saw as much combat in the

First World War as any American. The subject of war enters his hard, spare, singularly beautiful poems only in disguise, well camouflaged. Only a veteran could have written them. I doubt very much if any of the American poets who survived World War II experienced as much sustained and intense combat as Richard Wilbur. And, indeed, he has written (in a clipped, tight-lipped veteran's tone) a few of the most powerful poems of that war. But the subject of war has never been, explicitly, the burden of his poetry. Most often, and quite properly, it is those who stand between the civilian and the committed common soldier who are best able to translate the experience of war into a sensible affective language.

The poems in this book are inevitably mixed and uneven. They are consistent in telling the truth, though, and all belong—each must be here. There are, of course, more than enough good poems (as poems) to justify the book and the best attention any reader can bring. But ordinary judgment must be suspended. We are too close, and the wounds and scars, literal and metaphorical, are too fresh. These poems should not be taken or judged individually, but always in a sense of the experience of the whole book. We come to admire the poetry of this poem and that one in due time, but first we must experience them all. The single poems are parts of a larger, imagined and imaginary poem. They ask for and deserve the active and engaged imagination of the reader.

D.C. Berry may live to write many fine poems, even

"better" poems, as he grows and changes. But there is no denying his achievement here. He has done something once and for all. He has found the ways and means of telling the truth about his own war. He has been able to express the enormity of that experience and to summon up, in the ancient traditions of elegy, the pity of it all. In that sense this is an important book. It asks much of us and rewards us with more instruction than delight, but above all it offers an *experience* and, again as from the beginnings of our poems and history, an occasion to remember what we ought not to forget.

George Garrett

Hollins College, Virginia
February 1971

saigon cemetery

❦

The sun   goes
        down
a different way when

                   you
are lungshot in a rice
paddy and you
are taking a drink of
your own unhomeostatic
globules each

Time

you swallow a pail
of air   pumping like you
were

bailing out the whole
world   throw
   ing it in your leak
   ing   collapsible lung
that won't hold even
a good quart   and on
top of that   the sun
goes down

     Bang

ing the lung completely
flat.

3

Sometimes the tunnels
go empty
in the earth
when the Cong aren't
in them and the GI's haven't
found them and filled them full of
mother
earth.
then
the tunnel rats lie on their stomachs
and wonder what
an unfulfilled woman
does
with her
herself.

Go brood boy
        against the   mountains
and ask where their blood is gone
and their cuckoo song
sung
        in the spring once
once-upon-a-time
            boy. . . .

look into the pit
face   (many pitted
pock face   chiprutted with rock,
brown upon greenthough)
and shudder softshock against
the feel of its thousand
softgreen eternal unfocused
eyes upon you. and what are you

listening to when the bangle
rooster   crows   across
a water at you?

then hear the cricket's mighty rattle
rattle   rattle rattle
against your ear drumdrumdrumdrum
drum   machine gun
roar   gut gut gut gut gutgut   gut
        and down you go   boy
bloodclump
        dumped in a manufacturer's
rubber bodybag   and packed
home in a plane's metal belly
(against your jellybelly) cold
within the sack and given
back to a puzzled mother
who keeps foldingup and unfoldingup
the Bill of Lading.

❦

A yellow piece
        of the yellowmoon
was hacked off
into my
hand to munch
        at the war
coldcoffee   call.

        I ate instead
a piece of my? thumb
and gave the yellow
piece of   yellowmoon
to the Fat General

        who ate
it with metalyellow
gold DA
        molars/and/canines
smiling. . . .

        (if I
knew the difference
between the two
bites
I could turn the
world.)

They say Spring came
        in May when it came   may
be.   but a boy was dead then
        shot in the gut and gray
liver   by   the victor
Charley.

the boy's pa couldn't under
stand   spring killin
        of his boy—

"My God may
be he ain't really dead."
buried in the May
mound in the Cemetery.

the boy's ma said may
be   he's one of the Lord's
pretty flowers'll rise
resurrection day—
        "God woman ain't
no dead bulb gonna rise this May
never! God
        pity you Martha!"

8

❀

An airplane   jets
                cross sky that
carries it
with its
        bellyload of dumbbombs til
the airplane   jets   in
        to a pock of
flak   flak flak   flak   that
flaks it

jetswatter

splat

the

jetplane

fumble/tumbles

down

like

a common house

fly.

❧

I would say
this   that
while the rockets
        and mortars
        were falling

in the special
        forces camp
ground for the first time
that the Montagnard fighting
        slope,
thinking Buddha
        had
        shit
a burst of farts
against his temples,

died inclined,

his gasp too quick
for a dramatist
to do.

The perfume on the Oriental
        morning
blows from the broken flowers
taken
        from their roots by the

mourning   mamasan—

        lies
upon my nose's   tongue

like a sweet monsoon
with no flood to perform
nor despair to flood.

        the mamasan
walking about the dawn
as if   the message lately received
        has broken her body
        from its root—
walks
stiff
as on her
knees instead of her feet.

she drops an herb
in the ancient vase
to heal the death
of the flowers   hers

must grow more before

it dies.

❀

Tanks fret to tread out
at night and pitch
their hard   feeted
tracks   against the easy
vietnam plains   full
of   spider
     holes   because the
spiders have been known to
 eat

the   hard   toad
tanks   to
actually   de   feet

them   then they   die

in mechanical
jumps   till their several

patellas   pop.

To Terri
  For Mother's Day
  From Vietnam

                  I
Womb an almost-melted   jelloroom
named Mother
              or
mama   or mommy
              or
ma—womb too

circular to say with lips
      as baby,
and too slow say in
commerce/business. . . .

                  II
Mother
        the thing
        manchild
leaves   to cleave
        to her   semicompetitor
maker. . . .

          the thing
          womanchild
leaves—trading warmth
for hotwarmth. . . .

14

III

... woman's not made dust
(like man) but
                    ivorybone
strongstrong   to uphold
            the ancient not antique farm
that is tricked her
by plough

seed   on
seed then
                crop
child popped
out finally—   echoonly
left of motherscream   soon lost
in infant's   huge
lung   terror/trauma   cry....

IV

... it's said (can be said)
that mama's what
            neverstops
giving mama
            nevercuts
the coil of herself to
            herchild   (mr doctor
undoes the umbil   ical
with sterile quick   clip/snip)
            mama's what
nevernever stops
at all stops....

15

V

. . . old finally . . .
    mother of mother—
breasts   gonegone   to
    forgotten milkbottles
unpicked up . . .
      bursting
with fulfillment.
    she remembers she remembers
in the dimlight   the hotnights
      man's tongue   baby's gum. . . .

VI

Mother   sister
      of Earth:

      two pantries.

❦

Time gets on its Hobble
Feet and falls upon
its own

grittling kneefaces
       when you watch it—
leaving gray mental powder
on pastnow places. when

you don't watch

          it it
's

running pummeling pell
mell   hell

ter
   skel

ter

  like a thing

with fastsnake's feet that
either aren't or are

not seen in

Time.

17

The wind comes above   below   blow
ing   across/above the
helicopter   rotor/
blade that lays
upon the ground its blast
of rotor air
and   manybullets that
seek

without philosophy eek

life

              solving its problem
without answers.

Go catch a falling   burningstar
and give it to the Vietnamese Piers
Plowman peasant in the eternal
paddy kneedeep   .   .   .

he notices with antique eye soft
        as strange glass
that the   burningstar   doesn't last
like everlasting rice
and gives it back.

        tell him it is rice given
from heaven.   .   .   .

He will throwup the
antique eyes
 at you
knowing rain
can't
rainup.

❦

Lightning reaching out with electric
        wrinkles etches
insanely against the
        negronight
the inaccuracy of broken
        nerves
cracked across a moon
less sky and ripped
        of insensitivity.

The GI flys his phantom, craft
        ing in
air the map's frenzy
of
earth reaching with insensitive
radar fingers
for
the unbroken bridge
clinging across a
mapwrinkle.

The bridge and night gone;
the lightning committed
to the Transmission Wire Asylum
and the Phantom
asleep on safe
rubber wheels.

Positioned around the square

                    table
—four soldiers
positioned
behind   cards (never up side down)
looking across their   skyline. . . .

accoutered on each leftflank by a cold

                           sud
and on the flank(right) left
by a clear glass
        bowl
holding clean white tubes
of
      cigarettes burning themselves.

all quiet but
for facile conversation as the cards are
shotsoftly   cartwheel
at the tabletop.

The bay has green colors for
a face and spittles
     salt sting
from its Oriental
     face
of forever—

         yet the days
crawl across
       it
on waterbug legs
     that don't even
        tinydent
the waterface.

❦

The onehundred and
twentytwo   Milli
        meter   rocke
            t
halfcircling   its halfmoon
circle   halfcircles
        into the Past
Midnight Army bunker—

        eclipsing quickly
the hobbled timeroar
of a Timex Electric Wrist
Watch   crushing   it
perfectly   from

timekeeper
to timekept.

Tangerines and white
marshmallows pop before the
soldier's eyesbriefly   with the pop
of the AK-47
Assault Rifle's speedy mind
expanding bullet,

then a black canvas bag is stretched across
his thinking
and filled with hard
pieces of black chalk pieces
that powder slowly
with the bag as it relaxes
finally into dust

                    —closing Time
for

Forever.

The brownarmy chapel next
to the blue sky high with
heaven uphigh sits heavy squat ever
heaviness beside a black top heavy
road weariness
that runs dizzy
at the sky
where the horizon
lies like a knife edge upon
the world's
vision.

into outof the brown
army chapel soldiers come and go
with invisible brown grocery bags which
they carry   infull   outfull
of candy bars
sweet as sinsin
bitter as woe
that they wont
rip
out of the brown grocery
bag with the
knife
off the chaplain's hip.

❊

Now this doctor colonel fat
as a fatslaughtered lamb
felt
compelled
        to operate
a battalion sized battalion
like an army
commander. . . .

(time)

the doctor captains hat
        ed him so much that
they slaughtered him like a fat
lamb   one quarter
by not hiding his mistakes
        in cancer or formal
de hyde.

        actually the cap
tains just put him up
like meat on the table and
the fat colonel butcher cut
his own very birdballs off
proving evermore his
        eunuchness.

❀

The night has gone mad
drunk on Buddha's rottenwine rice:
　　　storming!
forming white balls of ice
on the camouflage
covered helmet
knowing
all the time that the
　　　head inside is
a dead Masterpiece
Oval....

then the white balls of ice
go down on cold waves
and be water
in the ground
　　　uncaught
by the oval helmet
fresh full of the de
warming GI head.

　　　the day comes
with its clear
insanity . . . only the oval
helmet remaining solid . . .
the head going
to putty.

The gasping redness touches
out of the gunmouth
        blasting wretchedness
death   making
        zeros
counted one
        by the
death editing
lieutenants—

        the numbers easily
covering all the bodies
on paper pale
        as/with
death and thin
        as
horizon.

The patient sleep
comes   that never becomes
impatient
            till the resurrection

awakens

in the Bible

        that lifts

        Earth's

dress up

and lets her bodies

        come out.

❦

This is the end where the begin
ning starts with the zing
  ing   unacrobatic

              bullet

that knows
that it is more

absolute

Algebra than Calculus,

nevertheless
northemore

it knows
              that when the wind
stops blowing by it

that it
is at

              the end

where
absolute
zero

begins
to
begin

30

❁

At dusk when Buddha begins mix
ing   up the darkoils   for
the black canvas

        he   jars
awake the   beensleeping swallows
who come out and   jet
   jetting away

jet/jet

senseless peasant insects
        indiscriminantly

        till Buddha throws
the darkoils out on the
canvas   coloring the swallow's red

eye   black   unabling him to

indiscriminate the
        peasant insects
discriminantly

(thus the jet
jetting about Buddha's
    black   canvas
         painted
blood   red   in

              sun

and black   in

              moon

like the swallow's   eye

at change).

What will we do
when we're done
with civilization.
when we're done

maybe we'll
find out that we're
      really caterpillars
looking for our cocoon

maybe we'll
find out that we're
      butterflies
dazed

by
the
Crack of Fall.

I said to the Earth
where Whore!
did you get your
Asian   African   European   American
children
from   from

under circus riders?   or
did you

contort with gymnasts?   .   .   .

Anyway
you
should find their fathers
and tell them how their kids
love to kill
more than love   at least.

tell their fathers that

all the arms of
Man must be

broken now!

The dark mountains   rise
        (mystery
in the skies ten
miles high
in Orient ink
black as a
Vietdame's harlot
        bought hair
hung down to her thumbed
        navel

black as a
Vietdame's harlot
        bought hair
down to her thumbed
        navel

        but
not black as her mystery
sold for retail!)
black as the Vietdame
Virgin who waits like
        a mustard seed
                for them to be crushed
by her
glacier of Hope.

❁

The thing about   A
bomb   is its appearance
in appearing singular
when it's
        really very
plural.

Now This
is the thing:

        it Fools You,
Downright Fools! You,
No ...
No, it doesn't Fool You

it Fools You All

No, it Fools US
and the USSR
and us ALL.

Now this is it Absolute:

it only   foolsfools.

❀

Clocks don't
work overtime   there's

too much Time

for that so
        they loaf

as though they
needed a   second   hand or
a   third   though
        they don't   they

loaf

eating caterpillars   (wasting them)
before they become   beautiful   butter
flies—caring that
        much for Future   they

don't

really care
that much
  Eating Them ! ! !

❦

If I'm zapped   bury me
with a
comicbook   let

Tennyson keep his
buried William Shakespeare   put

a comic
on my   chest   and   shovel
me   overtight

        in my new life I'll be

Clark Kent

instead
of

Superman.

❀
To Terri
    For Easter
    From Vietnam

This Morning   I   wake up
and find you sleeping at my side   sleeping
       as   earth
herself.

hardly noise   I lift from the bed
and see
       in the mirror me
and your night clothes
on the otherside of the bedding
and I laugh at the Thing
woman is but you don't hear.

I'm gone
from your very early morning
smell   of silence
into the woods where
behind the house behind
the mountain
where the flowers are awake
with early Easter. . . .

I go to pick one
for thee

(a flower must be killed only for
thee, never for a you).

the flower is killed
with love as only lovers kill

and I bring to thee,

I enter the room and you turn
tornsleep-heavy to me
and ask where I've been
and 'why'
and 'why topick aflower?'
and 'forwho?'

'Thee? Thee? . . . for
me ! ! ! ! ?

and your arms
go up and pull me
downdown to you
where the world is heavy
and half asleep
and you don't look pretty

biting your lip to not
cry. . . .

and now crying easily
        the flower fallen almost
forgotten. . . .

40

The way popcorn   pops   is
the way punji sticks snap
into your skin and stab

pricking urine
into   cardiovascular
systems and apparatus
apparently
unorganizing then demonstrating
it.

            then you die
either from the spike,
the   p,
or the

sun gone to grain
expanding

in your eye.

❀

Dr. Zhivago
could I invite you in
for a toast
of blood and phlegm—

if you don't
like its   ungray/red   color
        butter
it yellow.

        it's not wine
so don't tinysip it
        but down it
as though you were the hole
        the Dead
Sea fills;

            perhaps you could propose the
toast; we flounder at that
and strangle, our teeth
catching like crust against
words.

❦

If the man with the big spoon
would   spade
out
the   snake   sound
from Oriental music
        perhaps
we could all ride   not unlike
jockeys
        the marmalade music back into
the marshmallow garden
        (presently dirty
        dropped in the dirt)
of Adam and Eden
        —or was
it Adam and Eve?
        Oh God we
are lost?

Saigon's a good place to be
shot
at these days—

the VC's
Forward Artillery Observer:
        The Armed Forces Radio,
will tell you this at

1200hours & 1800hours

        between bursts of

rock and roll and soul
music,
        when
they tell how

close the rockets came

at 1200hours and

how much closer they came
at 1800hours
        bursting
        rudely

in spasms
of James Brown
Soul.

❀

At Dak To Casey Jones
was killed in a gunship
which in a hurry he let whirr
hot-throttle into Hill 919.

Remembering the rust on the
Rock Island Line boxcars,
he wished he could rust,
rust rather than rot, to rust
and rest in the iron tracks
and not be turned indiscriminantly
by an easy
worm.

Before dawn when the attack came
behind the mortars,
Lt. Donne rolled-up himself
into a globe
and spun-up into the safe sphere
of his canvas-covered steel
helmet   not fear
ing the sharp singing zing
of the hot-planet bullets
doing hyperbolas around his charming
microcosmicness.

Defying finally, however,
Captain Kepler's
lawful orders to stay in the exact
tract of his special trench,
he raised up from his
uniqueness
for a quick look and quickly faced

a 20 mm red-tailed tracer
tearing like a comet into his face
(to the effect
of fully erasing his space).

Sgt. Sam Sublime never died
when he was killed cause he kept
his heart in a blue
guitar. Snapped.

And I know cause I know
exactly where he was when
he put himself like a big black
beautiful bomb into that blue guitar
and got down on God!
Amighty! Got
down on a loin funky nigger
song that drove the snakes
in Oriental music   crazy.

And we would sit there holding on
to the Orient till our pulses
fell in with slow zooms in the
silent pounding of his song
and then we were gone where our ankles
weren't afraid of stepping on neither
the razor/horizon nor a booby
trap trip wire—

                    dancing like
an OD Caterpillar
in Sam's blood ballad
where we were safe from the
gooks and snakes.

Till a string broke
and they mailed Sam
home. Said
his spinal chord was
knocked completely out of tune
by the whack of a 10,000
pound bomb
from a B-52.

❀

Miss Flannery O'Connor,
I
went down
down to Saigon cemetery
and
found you sitting
as usual
casual about death.
> your tongue gone
> black chalk
> finger
> clapper in an empty
> broken bell on a gray
> stone.
Empty fruit jars
strewn about.

Not your jars they say,
for you had only a
dark jar
and there are several clear
Masons here.

A poem ought to be a salt lick
rather than sugar candy.
A preservative.
Something to make a tongue
tough enough to taste
the full flavor
of beauty and grief.

I would go to the dark
places where the
animals go;

they know
where the salt licks are
far
away from the barbed glitters of neon,
far
away from the bottles of booze
stacked like loaded rifles,
far
away into the gray-bone and
bleached silence.

I would go there now
before the slow explosion of Spring.
Already my tongue bleeds from
the yellow slash of Forsythia
that must be blooming
where you are.

50